SOUTH KOREA
WORLD ADVENTURES
BY HARRIET BRUNDLE

KidHaven PUBLISHING

Published in 2019 by
KidHaven Publishing, an Imprint of Greenhaven Publishing, LLC
353 3rd Avenue, Suite 255, New York, NY 10010

© 2019 Booklife Publishing

This edition is published by arrangement with Booklife Publishing.

Designer: Natalie Carr
Editor: Charlie Ogden
Writer: Harriet Brundle

Names: Brundle, Harriet.
Title: South Korea / Harriet Brundle.
Description: New York : KidHaven Publishing, 2019. | Series: World adventures | Includes index.
Identifiers: ISBN 9781534526204 (pbk.) | 9781534526198 (library bound) | ISBN 9781534526211 (6 pack) | ISBN 9781534526228 (ebook)
Subjects: LCSH: Korea (South)–Juvenile literature.
Classification: LCC DS907.4 B77 2019 | DDC 951.95–dc23

Printed in the United States of America

CPSIA compliance information: Batch # BS18KL: For further information contact Greenhaven Publishing LLC, New York, New York at 1-844-317-7404.

CONTENTS

Words in **red** can be found in the glossary on page 24.

WHERE IS SOUTH KOREA?

South Korea is a small country found in the eastern part of Asia.

ASIA

SOUTH KOREA

The **population** of South Korea is over 50 million people. The capital city of South Korea is called Seoul.

SEOUL, SOUTH KOREA

WEATHER AND LANDSCAPE

During the summer, South Korea is usually very hot with lots of rain. In the winter, the weather is usually much colder.

The South Korean landscape includes lots of hills, mountains, and rivers. The highest mountain in South Korea is called Hallasan Mountain.

HALLASAN MOUNTAIN, SOUTH KOREA

CLOTHING

HANBOK

Hanbok is the **traditional** style of dress worn in South Korea. It is usually bright and colourful.

People in South Korea usually wear comfortable and **modern** clothing.

RELIGION

The **religion** with the most followers in South Korea is Christianity. Many other people follow Buddhism.

Buddhism began over 2,500 years ago. A Buddhist place of **worship** is called a temple.

BUDDHIST TEMPLE, SOUTH KOREA

FOOD

KIMCHI

There are over 180 different varieties of kimchi.

Kimchi is a very popular dish in South Korea. It is usually made from cabbage, radishes, or cucumbers.

Many South Korean meals come with several small bowls of food called side dishes.

AT SCHOOL

Children in South Korea usually go to school when they are six years old. Children can leave school at fifteen years old, but most stay on until they are eighteen.

Many children in South Korea go to extra classes after school and over the weekend.

AT HOME

HANOK

The traditional style of house in South Korea is called hanok. Houses in this style have wing-like roofs and are usually made from wood.

When having a meal in a South Korean home, it is polite to try some of every dish and to finish all of the food on your plate.

FAMILIES

Family is a very important part of South Korean life. Children usually care for their parents and grandparents as they get older.

Children, parents, and grandparents often live together in the same house.

SPORTS

TAE KWON DO

Martial arts are very popular in South Korea.
The most popular type is called tae kwon do.

Baseball and Table Tennis are both very popular sports in South Korea. Children often play them after school.

BASEBALL

FUN FACTS

South Korea is home to lots of different animals, including the Asian black bear and the Korean magpie.

Once a year, South Korea holds a mud **festival** where people can take part in many different sports in the mud!

GLOSSARY

festival time when people come together to celebrate a special event

martial arts sports that involve self-defense or attacking with the hands or feet

modern something from recent or present times

population the number of people living in a place

religion the belief in and worship of a god or gods

traditional ways of behaving that have been done for a long time

worship a religious act such as praying

INDEX